NARC MOTHERS

MW01202040

An Healing Guide for Adult Children on How to Deal with a Narcissistic Personality

CATHERINE KING

TABLE OF CONTENTS

INTRODUCTION

If you have decided to purchase and read this book, you probably already know what narcissism is. However, most people don't actually know the origins of narcissism and its dictionary definition. The definition of narcissism is the pursuit of gratification through getting egotistic or vanity admiration of a person's idealized self-image. This encompasses arrogance, perfectionism, and self-flattery. The term 'narcissism' actually came from Greek mythology, where Narcissus saw his own face reflected in water and fell in love with himself. Sigmund Freud heavily uses the story of Narcissus in his written works. Eventually, the American Psychiatric Association classified narcissism as a personality disorder and can now be medically diagnosed.

Narcissism exists at every corner in life. Whether it's your boss, your friend, your grandfather, or your mother, you probably know a narcissist or two. Some narcissists are aware of the fact that they are suffering from this personality disorder but some have no idea. Their victims also may have no idea that they are being harmed by a narcissist. In this book, we will be exploring the basics of narcissism but we will primarily focus on narcissism within mothers. If a person grew up being raised by a narcissist, most of the time they may not realize it as they have nothing else to compare it. They may only start to realize the differences of their upbringing later on in life when they start to notice the many behavioral problems they have developed through being raised in a narcissistic environment. For instance, children raised by narcissistic parents may grow up wondering why they are such people pleasers and have trouble saying 'no.' Or they may wonder how other people can put themselves first whereas they were always conditioned to put a certain person's feelings and needs before their own.

Most people who grow up in a narcissistic

environment tend to have various self-esteem issues. In many serious cases, children who were raised by parents that were narcissistic tend to develop mental disorders such as anxiety and depression later on in life combined with low self-esteem. Encountering narcissism as a child versus as an adult has drastic differences.

Over the past decade, the term narcissist has been increasingly used according to Google Trends. Often times, the word 'narcissist' is used as an insult. Nobody wants to be called a narcissist or to have someone imply that you are one. However, everybody has their own narcissistic needs; this is normal. In order to have a healthy self-esteem, people need to be praised and encouraged by their parents and caregivers. If this isn't done, children normally grow up with low self-esteem. Sigmund Freud suggested that everyone has to go through a stage called 'primary narcissism.' This is the primitive state of mind that everyone goes through when they can't understand that other people are separate beings. Other philosophers and professionals in this area believed that people who suffered from narcissism disorders could be caused by the way their parents raise them. If parents undervalued their children, they grow up to have low self-esteem whereas if parents overvalued their children, they could grow up to have too high of a self-esteem which could cause narcissistic disorders. Some theories also suggest that there is no such thing as self-esteem that is 'too high.' Instead, people who are over-confident likely are putting on a mask or a front to hide their low self-esteem. An interesting theory that's been suggested has stated that people who have narcissistic personalities get the validation that they need from other people and by boosting themselves as much as they can. By convincing themselves that they are great, they are actually building artificial confidence which typically leaves a narcissist with no way to support their own claims and self-esteem.

In order to truly heal and escape from narcissism in your life, you must have a strong understanding of what it is, the different types, and many other facets. This book will serve as a tool for you to learn about narcissism in-depth so you can escape if forever. This book will begin with a chapter that surrounds the basics of narcissism. We will learn about the science behind it, the different types of narcissism, how narcissism manifests in society, and what the symptoms are. After that, we will be taking a look into the 16 different personality types and which ones are more prone to narcissism. We will also take a look into personality disorders and their different types and which narcissism falls into. After that, we will be taking a deeper look into narcissistic personality disorders, its causes and symptoms. This will help you identify whether or not you are dealing with a narcissist in your life. We will also cover the topics of diagnosing narcissistic personality disorders and treatments for people who have it. Towards the meat of the book, we will be studying manipulation techniques that narcissists use. We will learn about how narcissists strategize their manipulation to control people. After that, we will be studying narcissism specifically in family environments. We will take a look at the common dynamics of a family that has a narcissist. In our case, we will be studying the dynamics of a family that has a narcissistic mother. We will then spend a chapter learning about codependency as families that have a narcissist tend to become codependent on one another for support. This will help you understand if your relationships with other family members may be unhealthy due to the coping mechanisms used to deal with the narcissist. After that, we will be spending an entire chapter studying narcissism in mothers. You will learn how to recognize if you have a narcissistic mother, different types, behaviors, and the effects that it has on children. In our last chapter, we will learn about growing up in a narcissistic family and the effects it has on children. This book will effectively set you up with the right knowledge to fully understand everything behind the mind of a narcissist. In the second book of the series, we will focus on protecting yourself from a narcissist and how   to   heal   from   one.

CHAPTER 1

A NARCISSISTIC MOTHER

In this chapter, we are going to look at narcissism and how it can affect the children of a narcissistic mother.

What is a Narcissistic Mother

Previously in this book, we have discussed the makings and attributes of a narcissist so that you are now well-equipped to tell if someone with whom you are interacting is a narcissist. We are going to delve into this topic deeper now and discuss narcissism from the lens of a child with a narcissistic mother. To begin, what is a narcissistic mother? A narcissistic mother is one that requires validation. A narcissistic mother will not see their child for who they are but instead a projection of themselves in their child. This includes their hopes and expectations as well as what they hope to gain through this child.

How to Recognize if You Have a Narcissist Mother

It can be quite difficult to determine if you have a narcissistic mother. It is difficult to look at something as close as your own family member from a critical perspective in order to determine if she is in fact a narcissist. In this section, we will look at some signs that you can observe in order to recognize your own mother for who she may be- a narcissist. Below, we will look at some signs of a narcissistic mother and how you can tell if your mother is a narcissist.

1. Appears Perfect on the Outside

The narcissistic mother appears to others outside of the family to have it all together. She has a great job, a good amount of money, she serves on the school council or takes field trips with her children's class, she is involved in the lives of her children as she takes them to gymnastics or hockey practice, waving hello to all of the other parents. She places high importance on appearing successful and achieving those envious looks of approval and jealousy that she gets from the other parents. She loves the attention that these things bring her. She places high importance on her looks- both physically and her overall appearance of success.

2. Self- Centered

This type of mother is very focused on herself, even more than she is on her children. She is focused on her needs and her desire for attention and validation above everything else. This does not change regardless of the age of her children or the number of children she has.

3. Easily-Angered

If things do not work as she expected them to, or if she is not receiving the amount of attention that she desires, this type of woman will become angry and will lash out at her children verbally. There is nothing that causes this to happen the majority of the time, other than the fact that she feels deserving of more attention or validation than she is receiving.

4. Always Right

The narcissistic mother is always right. She is never able to admit that she may be in the wrong and is unable to accept that she has ever made a mistake. They have great difficulty with the words "I'm sorry," and you will likely never hear them uttered from her mouth. If you challenge her or tell her that she is wrong, she will become angry and confrontational. She cannot bear to think that she has been mistaken.

5. You Feel as Though you Must Walk on Eggshells

When it comes to the above traits, you may be able to argue that many women possess these traits- such as placing importance on their beauty or appearing to have a lot of money. The difference is that women who are not narcissistic will put these things aside when they have kids, recognizing that it is now their responsibility to take care of the needs of their children. They recognize that it is their job to support and nurture their children. Narcissistic mothers, however, maintain their need for control, approval and attention even after they have children. They begin to control their children and demand attention from them, instead of giving their attention to the children.

Different Types of Narcissistic Mothers

There are different types of narcissistic mothers, and knowing the different types will help you to determine if you have a narcissistic mother.

The Flamboyant-Extrovert

This is the type of narcissistic mother, which we often see on the television or in the movies. This type enjoys being an entertainer in public and is loved by those who know her out in the world. However, secretly, she is feared by her children and her partner. This type is the one that would be the stage mom, pushing her children to be better and better while also appearing to be involved and invested in their lives. She is all about performing, as this brings her the attention she craves. This type is extroverted and commands the attention of many with her loud and flashy gestures and tone of voice. The people who do not know her well enough love her, but her children despise the facade she puts on for the world. Her children don't really matter to her and are only playing a part in her show, as they inform how she looks to the outside world.

The Accomplishment-Oriented

This type of narcissistic mother is the type that places their children's accomplishments above everything else. To her, her child's success depends on what they manage to do, and not who they are as a person. This mom focuses heavily on college acceptances, grades, and degrees. The problem is, when they do not accomplish what she wants them to, she becomes gravely embarrassed, and she may also become angry and verbally abusive. To her, your success is a reflection of her.

The Psychosomatic

This narcissistic, psychosomatic mother uses her own aches, pains, and illnesses as a way of manipulating other people, in order to get her way, as well as to gain attention from as many people as she can. She does not care about those around her. Instead, she cares about the attention she can get from them. Children learn quickly that they get attention from this type of mother by taking care of her physical needs. This type of narcissistic mother uses her supposed illnesses to escape her feelings and escape having to deal with any difficulties that occur in her life. This type of mother will always be the sickest. Nobody is able to beat her when it comes to illness and pains, as she will always have something else to beat your level of sickness.

The Addicted

This narcissistic mother has problems with substance abuse, and this comes across as extremely narcissistic, as her addiction will always be her number one priority. It speaks louder than anything and anyone else. There are some instances when this type of mother may seem less narcissistic when they become sober- if they do, but this is not always the case, they may be a narcissist even behind the substance abuse. The substance that they are addicted to is always their choice before and above the needs of their child.

The Secretly Mean

This mother is secretly mean, as she does not want people outside of the immediate family to know that she is narcissistic and, therefore abusive to her children. This type of narcissistic mother has a public image and a very different private image or personality. This type of mother is loving, happy and kind to her children in public, but she is cruel and abusive in the home. The way that she sends very opposite messages to her children in and out of the home makes them feel crazy and anxious, as it is so unpredictable for the child.

The Emotionally Needy

It is a characteristic of narcissistic mothers to be emotionally needy, but this type specifically displays this characteristic in a much more open and obvious way than other types of narcissistic mothers. This type of narcissistic mother wants their children to take care of their emotional needs, which is a losing game for the child. This is because there is no importance placed on the child's feelings, and instead, the child is expected to give to their mother while never receiving anywhere close to the same level of nurturance as they give to their mother.

A narcissistic mother may fall into multiple categories, or she may fit best into just one of them. Everyone is different, and the type of maternal narcissism that she exhibits may be quite personal to her. You may find some of the above categories to resonate with you.

Behaviors of a Narcissistic Mother

We will now look at some of the most telltale signs of a narcissistic mother and how they are manifested in daily life with her.

Lacking Patience

In addition to the five most common behaviors of a narcissistic mother as described above, one of the major signs is that they lack patience. When it comes to having children, patience is key. Children have many needs that they are unable to take care of themselves and being patient through this is absolutely necessary. Further, children are unable to communicate their needs in a way that adults are able to understand for the first year or so of their lives. Patience is required during these stages especially in order to learn and understand how to read your children's actions and noises.

Lacking Empathy

Another one of the biggest signs of a narcissistic mother is that they lack empathy. When having children or any other intimate relationships, having empathy is very necessary. This is because children will often push their parent's buttons and try to get away with many naughty behaviors. If a parent is unable to be empathetic to these behaviors and is unable to understand a child's motivation by practicing empathy, they will become angered quickly. Children will often demand things and will need things immediately as they ask for them, such as going to the toilet. Having empathy means that you understand that needing to go to the toilet is an uncomfortable feeling and you will likely act quickly in order to help them feel better. Without empathy in this situation, a mother would instead become angry and annoyed and would likely yell at her child or deny them their needs as it is inconvenient for the mother and her own needs, which in her eyes, come first and foremost.

The Effects of a Narcissistic Mother on Their Children

There are many effects that having a narcissistic mother has on children. These negative effects are far-reaching and are long-lasting as the brains of children are still developing and are very receptive to the behavior and patterns that are modeled for them. They learn quickly how to deal with their parents and how to accommodate in order to make the entire environment of their house more peaceful.

When children are mothered by a narcissist, the children will often please in order to simply avoid the rage that would follow if they did not. They do so at the expense of themselves and their own needs. They learn quickly that if they engage in a fight with her, there is no chance of winning. She will not quit until you tell her she is right, and she has won, as she cannot stand being told she is wrong. She is desperate to win every argument, even if it is with her own child. Thus, you decide not to engage.

When you are little, you are taught to listen to and respect the adults in your life, as they know more than you, and you are only there to listen and learn. This is even more extreme when the main adult in your life is a narcissistic mother. As you grow up, you learn that you must listen to your mother and make her comfortable in order to be shown some love. You learn that if you take care of their every need, you may receive a small sliver of love from her. Since you know that you are not old enough to take care of yourself, you know that you need her. Since you need her, you greatly value the small amounts of love that she gives to you. They are few and far between, but they are necessary for you. You continue to make her happy and avoid angering her at all costs in order to receive this. The problem is, she is very quick to anger and thus many times she will become angry despite your best efforts to keep her happy. You then tell yourself that you are not doing a good enough job pleasing her or that you must have done something wrong. This makes you feel anxious when you are around her, as you know that despite your best efforts, sometimes she becomes angry anyway.

This leads children to become anxious and unsettled even in their own home. It leads to feelings of instability in the home, and this is unfair to a child, as they are still learning and growing, and this type of behavior is confusing for their developing brains. Instead of making you feel unstoppable and capable in the world, she ignites feelings of self-doubt within you from an early age since nothing meets her standards.

There is a term called psychological whiplash. This is something that is experienced by children of narcissistic mothers. Psychological whiplash is when a child is being thrown back and forth by the rage and the small offers of love. If they hold back their attention to her needs in response to her rage, they are met with more rage. If they put themselves aside to please her, they are met with small offers of love. As soon as something sets her off, though, she is raging again, without warning. The narcissistic mother is controlling in her use of withdrawal as a looming threat if she does not get what she wants, or the looming threat of an outburst.

Sons of Narcissistic Mothers

Sons of narcissistic mothers learn that they must do everything their mother wants and needs, trying to keep her happy in order to receive even an ounce of maternal love. As a result, they often come across as "momma's boys" and appear to be overly attached to their mother. This is only because they need the love that she dishes out in very small portions, and they must be there for when she decides to give it out. These men (if they are heterosexual) will often end up with a partner who is demanding and attention-seeking just like their mother in adulthood since they only know how to try to please a woman. The other option is that they become narcissistic themselves as they learned that their mother got what she wanted through her ways of relating to others and they continue to try to appear successful on the outside in order to receive validation from their mother, but they lack empathy as they never learned how to develop it.

Daughters of Narcissistic Mothers

The daughters of narcissistic mothers often find themselves being seen as an extension of their mother and her need for attention. They often find themselves being criticized by her and themselves for not being thin enough, pretty enough, smart enough, involved enough, and so on. The narcissistic mother also needs to be the most successful though. Thus, she may begin to compete with her daughter if she feels that the daughter is taking the attention away from her by being too successful or too pretty or anything like this. Because the daughter already has the advantage of having youth, she is jealous of this. The position that this puts the daughter in is a confusing one, as she is both criticized for being too good and not good enough at the same time. The daughter is never allowed to be her own individual and has never been appreciated for who she is, which leads to decreased self-esteem and feelings of low self-worth.

As they age, daughters of narcissistic mothers may become pleasers and become partners of men who are unappreciative of them, which reenacts their childhood where they never felt good enough. They may feel depression and anxiety as a result of this, due to the fact that they have never had their needs met by themselves or by anyone else. The daughters of narcissistic mothers continue to seek validation as they have never received it. They may chase riches and have multiple procedures in an effort to be pretty enough. They cannot find love for themselves as they tied their self-worth to the validation they hoped to receive from their mother, that never came.

The Pleasing Father

The father in this situation goes along with everything, as he is just as scared and intimidated as the children are. Instead of standing up to his wife as an equal, he pleases her as well. Instead of taking care of his children's needs, he is occupied with the needs of his wife as he risks rage, withdrawal from the relationship, or being kicked out altogether if he does not. He does not feel worthy enough to stand up or get out and this pattern continues for as long as the mother wants- which is often a long time as she is getting what she wants.

The narcissistic mother was not born in this way. She likely developed these traits as a result of her own childhood and the things she experienced. This does not make this behavior any better, but it makes it easier for her children to understand her in order to make peace with their own childhood and their mother.

CHAPTER 2

GROWING UP IN A NARCISSISTIC FAMILY

We have talked at length in this book so far about how having a narcissistic mother deeply affects her children and stays with them as they age. We have seen how her children can grow into pleasers, following their upbringing, or how they can grow into narcissists themselves as a result of overly identifying with their mother. In this chapter, we are going to look at how to break this before it informs these children's relationships and their feelings about themselves into adulthood. There is hope for children of narcissistic mothers to break away from the grasp of their mother and lead their own independent and healthy lives and relationships.

How to Break Away From Codependency Within the Family

When you realize that your family relationships are not healthy and are actually quite dysfunctional as a result of a narcissistic mother, it can be very difficult to break away from this. The patterns within a codependent family unit are solidified and are very sensitive to change. It can seem like there is no way to get out of this, but in this section, we will look at two ways to do this.

'No Contact'

The first method of breaking free of the codependency of the relationship with a narcissistic mother is to go "no contact." This method is able to be done once you are an adult child and have moved out of her home, or if you are living with your father post-divorce. This involves completely cutting off contact with your narcissistic mother. When undertaking this, there are some things that you must realize.

It will not be easy. This is by no means an easy decision, and you will likely jump back and forth for some time before deciding to do this. Regardless of how dysfunctional your relationship with your narcissistic mother, there will always be some part of you that wants her approval and her love, even if it is never coming. It will be difficult to decide to do this, but if you do, you must show yourself compassion and understanding as it will take some time to accept.

Another thing to keep in mind is that you cannot expect others to understand your decision. People see a child's relationship with their mother as the one that will never be broken, that is full of love and understanding. Many people do not understand narcissism or what it is like to grow up with a narcissistic parent, so they will not readily accept or understand why or how you decided to cut contact with your mother. Further, since she cannot see the error of her ways, she will not understand either. This is something that you will need to expect and move past, reminding yourself why you chose to make this decision and how it is better for your mental health in the long-run, even if it is hard at first.

'Ignoring Her Behaviors'

Another way that you can break free of the codependent relationship with your narcissistic mother is by ignoring her behaviors. The thought behind this method is that you will make yourself as emotionless and boring as you possibly can and avoid playing into the arguments or demands of your narcissistic mother. As a result of this, the mother will not be receiving the attention or validation that they so desperately crave, so they will go elsewhere to seek it. You avoid engaging in fights or responding to their demands and insults so that you do not get caught up in their vortex. In order to effectively use this method, you need to understand that you are not doing so in order to get revenge or closure out of it, or that the narcissistic mother will ever realize or apologize for their actions. This method will also be very difficult, but it can be effective when you have no other choice, such as if you must live with them or see them in certain situations (such as a funeral or something involving legal matters).

Where you can, cutting contact completely will be much harder but much more effective in the long-run. If you can use this method, it will leave you much more free than ignoring them will, but you must recognize that it will involve a grieving process and will require strong boundaries as well as compassion for yourself.

How to Avoid Codependency in Your Own Relationships

If a person grows up in a family with a narcissistic mother, their familial relationships are likely codependent in nature. As this is the only sort of relationship, you have had modeled for you, the chances of engaging in a codependent relationship later in life when you are choosing your own partner are high, as you do not know anything different. As children, the relationship that demonstrates to us how to conduct ourselves in our own personal relationships when we get older is that between our parents. If this relationship is unhealthy in any way, namely by being codependent, then we will go on to find ourselves in one later on in life.

1. Recognize

Recognizing these patterns is the first step in breaking the chain of codependency. By recognizing that you have only been shown a codependent relationship, you are welcoming the chance to learn and grow in a new and healthy way.

2. Prioritize Self-Care

Since codependent relationships involve a pleaser and a narcissist, you can break away from codependency by taking care of your needs instead of putting them aside in order to take care of your partner's needs. By sacrificing your own needs, you show the other person that you will put them above yourself. In order to break away from this, you must prioritize yourself and demonstrate to yourself and your partner that you are not willing to sacrifice yourself for anyone or anything. By practicing self-care, you are ensuring your own happiness, comfort, and health. Self-care practices can include getting adequate sleep, exercising, taking time to be alone, enjoying your own hobbies and so on.

3. Let the Other Person be Themselves

People who tend toward codependency often like to control others, which comes from a good place but can leave them feeling exhausted and burnt out. These people often want to control the actions or decisions of others in order to help them or lead them on a good path, but you must recognize that you cannot control others, and they are in control of their own choices and the consequences that result.

4. Give Yourself Validation

As people who grew up with narcissistic mothers tend to have a low level of self-worth or a negative self-image, they tend to seek validation by caring for others. In order to break free from codependency, it is important to validate yourself. This will reduce the need you feel to seek validation from others and will return your power back to you- instead of putting it in someone else's hands. You can do this by looking at your positive attributes, forgiving yourself for anything that you may need to notice your strengths and by reminding yourself that you are important and worthy of love without having to earn it.

5. Practice Compassion

Codependent people often judge and criticize themselves as they have extremely high expectations of themselves and blame themselves when something doesn't turn out as they wished or expected. This comes from a childhood where the expectation was perfection and then inevitable disappointment. Criticizing yourself only decreases your feelings of self-worth and it serves no good. In order to break this, you must treat yourself with the same empathy that you show to others when you are helping them or caring for them. You are deserving of your own love just like (or even more than) they are. Release yourself from the expectation of perfection and have compassion for yourself.

6. Ask for Help

It is very difficult for people who grew up with a narcissistic mother to ask for help, as they have always been the ones giving help, not receiving it. In order to break out of this, This also comes from the desire to appear strong and not weak, and viewing asking for help as weak. Asking for help is something that everyone needs to do sometimes and allowing yourself to do so will help you to break away from the role of a pleaser and attain a more even ground with your partner. A healthy relationship should involve giving and receiving.

7. Set Boundaries

This point is very important for pleasers as they have great difficulty setting boundaries. They are uncomfortable saying "no" and fear that this will lead a person to reject them. Having a healthy relationship involves having boundaries. Just as you would respect someone else's boundaries, you can expect others to respect yours. Setting a boundary could be anything that you expect or need from a relationship, or anything that you will not put up within a relationship. Everyone has things that are okay and that are not okay and it is your right to communicate this, especially in romantic relationships.

8. Be Assertive

Continuing from number seven above, it is important to be assertive when maintaining and establishing your boundaries. This is how you get people to respect them in, in turn, respect you. By not being assertive with your boundaries, people will not take them   seriously.

CHAPTER 3

USING COGNITIVE BEHAVIORAL THERAPY TO HEAL FROM NARCISSISM

Cognitive Behavioral Therapy is the most effective form of speaking therapy right now. It especially works to help victims of narcissism due to helping the victims change the way they perceive their thoughts. CBT's theory is that our thoughts affect our emotions which then affects our behaviors. The theory of CBT also talks about how our thoughts are simply just thoughts and can be changed if we actively tried to. People may not know it, but the patterns of our thoughts are developed through our experiences and conditioning. For instance, a victim of narcissism may always be having thoughts about how they are always wrong or they are not good enough in general. However, these thoughts usually have no supporting evidence, but yet, it still causes them a lot of emotional pain. CBT works in a way that it helps its patients figure out which of their thoughts actually are evidence-based and which are just developed through their own unhealthy thinking styles.

How Does Cognitive Behavioral Therapy Work?

Cognitive Behavioral Therapy works by emphasizing the relationship between our thoughts, feelings, and behaviors. When you begin to change any of these components, you start to initiate change in the others. The goal of CBT is to help lower the amount you worry and increase the overall quality of your life. Here are the 8 basic principles of how Cognitive Behavioral Therapy works:

1. CBT will help provide a new perspective of understanding your problems.

A lot of the times, when an individual has been living with a problem for a long time in their life, they may have developed unique ways of understanding it and dealing with it. Usually, this just maintains the problem or makes it worse. CBT is effective in helping you look at your problem from a new perspective, and this will help you learn other ways of understanding your problem and learning a new way of dealing with it.

2. CBT will help you generate new skills to work out your problem.

You probably know that understanding a problem is one matter, and dealing with it is entirely another can of worms. To help start changing your problem, you will need to develop new skills that will help you change your thoughts, behaviors, and emotions that are affecting your anxiety and mental health. For instance, CBT will help you achieve new ideas about your problem and begin to use and test them in your daily life. Therefore, you will be more capable of making up your own mind regarding the root issue that is causing these negative symptoms.

3. CBT relies on teamwork and collaboration between the client and therapist (or program).

CBT will require you to be actively involved in the entire process, and your thoughts and ideas are extremely valuable right from the beginning of the therapy. You are the expert when it comes to your thoughts and problems. The therapist is the expert when it comes to acknowledging the emotional issues. By working as a team, you will be able to identify your problems and have your therapist better address them. Historically, the more the therapy advances, the more the client takes the lead in finding techniques to deal with the symptoms.

4. The goal of CBT is to help the client become their own therapist.

Therapy is expensive; we all know that. One of the goals of CBT is to not have you become overly dependent on your therapist because it is not feasible to have therapy forever. When therapy comes to an end, and you do not become your own therapist, you will be at high risk for a relapse. However, if you are able to become your own therapist, you will be in a good spot to face the hurdles that life throws at you. In addition, it is proven that having confidence in your own ability to face hardship is one of the best predictors of maintaining the valuable information you got from therapy. By playing an active role during your sessions, you will be able to gain the confidence needed to face your problems when the sessions are over.

5. CBT is succinct and time-limited.

As a rule of thumb, CBT therapy sessions typically last over the course of 10 to 20 sessions. Statistically, when therapy goes on for many months, there is a higher risk of the client becoming dependent on the therapist. Once you have gained a new perspective and understanding of your problem, and are equipped with the right skills, you are able to use them to solve future problems. It is crucial in CBT for you to try out your new skills in the real world. By actually dealing with your own problem hands-on without the security of recurring therapy sessions, you will be able to build confidence in your ability to become your own therapist.

6. CBT is direction based and structured.

CBT typically relies on a fundamental strategy called 'guided recovery'. By setting up some experiments with your therapist, you will be able to experiment with new ideas to see if they reflect your reality accurately. In other words, your therapist is your guide while you are making discoveries in CBT. The therapist will not tell you whether you are right or wrong, but instead, they will help develop ideas and experiments to help you test these ideas.

7. CBT is based on the present, "here and now".

Although we know that our childhood and developmental history play a big role in who we are today, one of the principles of CBT actually distinguishes between what caused the problem and what is maintaining the problem presently. In a lot of cases, the reasons that maintain a problem are different than the ones that originally caused it. For example, if you fall off while riding a horse, you may become afraid of horses. Your fear will continue to be maintained if you begin to start avoiding all horses and refuse to ride one again. In this example, the fear was called by the fall, but by avoiding your fear, you are continuing to maintain it. Unfortunately, you cannot change the fact that you had fallen off the horse, but you can change your behaviors when it comes to avoidance. CBT primarily focuses on the factors that are maintaining the problem because these factors are susceptible to change.

8. Worksheet exercises are significant elements of CBT therapy.

Unfortunately, reading about CBT or going to one session of therapy a week is not enough to change our ingrained patterns of thinking and behaving. During CBT, the client is always encouraged to apply their new skills into their daily lives. Although most people find CBT therapy sessions to be very intriguing, it does not lead to change in reality if you do not exercise the skills you have learned.

These eight principles will be your guiding light throughout your Cognitive Behavioral Therapy. By learning, understanding, and applying these eight principles, you will be in a good position to invest your time and energy into becoming your own therapist and achieving your personal goals. Based on research, individuals who are highly motivated to try exercises outside of sessions tend to find more value in therapy than those who don't. Keep in mind that other external factors still have an effect on your success, but your motivation is one of the most significant factors. By following CBT using the principles above, you should be able to remain highly motivated throughout CBT.

When is Cognitive Behavioral Therapy Used?

Now that we have learned how CBT works, when is CBT used? The main answer to this question is that CBT is used when an individual decides to pursue therapy in order to help with the problems they are facing. A lot of the time, these problems are disorders such as depression, anxiety, or more serious ones like OCD and PTSD.

To dive a little more in-depth, the most common uses for CBT is actually depression and generalized anxiety disorder. However, CBT is also used and is very effective for other disorders such as:

- Body Dysmorphic Disorder
- Eating Disorders
- Chronic Low Back Pain
- Personality Disorders
- Psychosis
- Schizophrenia
- Substance Used Disorders

Since CBT focuses on the relationship between thoughts, emotions, and behavior, those who suffer from disorders that stem from mental health may find it helpful to try CBT. Most modern-day therapists opt for CBT as the best technique to handle the problems that the client may be facing as it covers numerous disorders, and the client can learn it and continue to use it without the therapist's help.

On a simpler note, CBT can just be used for general therapy. This may be a situation where somebody is attending therapy sessions in order to remain in touch with their thoughts and feelings. Although this person may not be suffering from any particular disorder, CBT is a helpful tool for someone who wants to organize their thoughts.

Who Uses Cognitive Behavioral Therapy?

A large variety of people use Cognitive Behavioral Therapy, whether it is to help others or to solve their own problems. The most general answer to who uses CBT would be a therapist and somebody who is suffering from a mental disorder. However, CBT is also used by professionals within the psychology space, alcohol addiction, substance abuse, eating disorders, phobias, and anger management. CBT is a flexible tool that many types of people can use to treat the problem at hand.

Like I mentioned in the previous subchapter,

CBT can be used even if you are not facing a serious problem like mentioned above. Many people who used to go to therapy continue to use CBT to maintain a healthy mindset. CBT has also been used for events like interventions. However, the people that typically use and gain the most from CBT are the people who are willing to spend the time and energy analyzing their own thoughts and feelings. Since self-analysis is typically difficult, a lot of people may give up after realizing how uncomfortable it could be. However, CBT is very well-suited for the people who are looking for short term treatment that does not require medication. This is very suitable for people who don't want to take drugs in order to manage disorders like depression and anxiety.

Unhelpful Thinking Styles

To effectively use CBT, you must understand the different types of cognitive distortions or otherwise known as 'unhelpful thinking styles'. By knowing what these different styles are, you are able to identify when it is happening and use CBT to change that thought/worry. By determining whether your worry is justified or not, you are able to control if you worry will then lead to anxiety. Below are the twelve types of cognitive distortions that you need to learn:

1. All or nothing thinking: This is otherwise known as 'black and white thinking'. You tend to see things in either black or white or success or failure. If your performance is not perfect, you will see it as a failure.

2. Overgeneralization: You see one single negative situation as a pattern that never ends. You draw conclusions of future situations based on one single event.

3. Mental filter: You choose one single undesirable detail, and you exclusively dwell on it. Your perception of reality becomes negative based on it. You only notice your failures, but you don't look at your successes.

4. Disqualifying the positive: You discount

your positive experiences or success by saying "that doesn't count". By discounting all your positive experiences, you can maintain a negative perspective even if it is contradicted in your daily life.

5. Jumping to conclusions: You make a negative assumption even when you don't have supporting evidence. There are two types of jumping to conclusions:

a. Mind reading: You imagine that you already know what other people are thinking negatively of you, and therefore you don't bother to ask.

b. Fortune-telling: You predict that things will end up badly, and you convince yourself that your prediction is a fact.

6. Magnification/Minimization: You blow things out of proportion or inappropriately shrink something to make it seem unimportant. For example, you beef up somebody else's achievement (magnification) and shrug off your own (minimization).

7. Catastrophizing: You associate terrible and extreme consequences to the outcome of situations and events. For example, if you are rejected for a date, it means that you are alone forever, and making an error at work means you will be fired.

8. Emotional reasoning: You make the assumption that your negative emotions reflect the reality. For example, "I feel it so, therefore, it is true".

9. "Should" statements: You motivate yourself using "shoulds" and "shouldn'ts" as if you associate a reward or punishment before you do anything. Since you associate reward/punishment with shoulds and shouldn'ts for yourself, when other people don't follow it, you feel anger or frustration.

10. Labeling and mislabeling: This is overgeneralization to the extreme. Instead of describing your mistake, you automatically associate a negative label to yourself "I'm a loser". You also do this to others. If someone else's behavior is undesirable, you attach "they are a loser" to them as well.

11. Personalization: You take responsibility for something that wasn't your fault. You see yourself as the cause of an external situation.

12. All at once, bias: This is when you think risks and threats are right at your front door, and the amount of it is increasing as well. When this occurs, you tend to:

a. Think that negative situations are evolving quicker than you can come up with solutions

b. Think that situations are moving so quickly that you feel overwhelmed

c. Think that there is no time between now and the impending threat

d. Numerous risks and threats seem to all appear at the same time

By understanding these cognitive distortions and unhelpful thinking styles, you will have the opportunity to interrupt the process and say, for example, "I'm catastrophizing again." When you are able to interrupt your own thinking styles that are not helping, you are able to readjust it to something that is more helpful. In the next chapter, we will be discussing some tips and tricks to help you challenge your own cognitive distortions. This is one of the main strategies within CBT.

Challenging Your Unhelpful Thinking Styles

Once you are able to identify your own unhelpful thinking styles, you can begin trying to reshape those thoughts into something more realistic and factual. In this chapter, I have categorized all the different cognitive distortions and what questions you should be asking yourself to develop different thoughts.

Keep in mind that it takes a lot of effort and dedication to change our own thoughts, so don't get frustrated if you are not succeeding right away. You probably have had these thoughts for a while, so don't expect it to change overnight.

Probability Overestimation

If you find that you have thoughts about a possible negative outcome, but you are noticing that you often overestimate the probability, try asking yourself the questions below to reevaluate your thoughts.

☐ Based on my experience, what is the probability that this thought will come true realistically?

☐ What are the other possible results from this situation? Is the outcome that I am thinking of now the only possible one? Does my feared outcome have the highest possible out of the other outcomes?

☐ Have I ever experienced this type of situation before? If so, what happened? What have I learned from these past experiences that would be helpful to me now?

☐ If a friend or loved one is having these thoughts, what would I say to them?

Catastrophizing

☐ If the prediction that I am afraid of really did come true, how bad would it really be?

☐ If I am feeling embarrassed, how long will this last? How long will other people remember/talk about it? What are all the different things they could be saying? Is it 100% that they will talk about only bad things?

☐ I am feeling uncomfortable right now, but is this really a horrible or unbearable outcome?

☐ What are the other alternatives for how this situation could turn out?

☐ If a friend or loved one was having these thoughts, what would I say to them?

Mind Reading

☐ Is it possible that I really know what other people's thoughts are? What are the other things they could be thinking about?

☐ Do I have any evidence to support my own assumptions?

☐ In the scenario that my assumption is true, what is so bad about it?

Personalization

☐ What other elements might be playing a role in the situation? Could it be the other person's stress, deadlines, or mood?

☐ Does somebody always have to be at blame?

☐ A conversation is never just one person's responsibility.

☐ Were any of these circumstances out of my control?

Should Statements

☐ Would I be holding the same standards to a loved one or a friend?

☐ Are there any exceptions?

☐ Will someone else do this differently?

All or Nothing Thinking

☐ Is there a middle ground or a grey area that I am not considering?

☐ Would I judge a friend or loved one in the same way?

☐ Was the entire situation 100% negative? Was there any part of the situation that I handled well?

☐ Is having/showing some anxiety such a horrible thing?

Selective Attention/Memory

☐ What are the positive elements of the situation? Am I ignoring those?

☐ Would a different person see this situation differently?

☐ What strengths do I have? Am I ignoring those?

Negative Core Beliefs

☐ Do I have any evidence that supports my negative beliefs?

☐ Is this thought true in every situation?

☐ Would a loved one or friend agree with my self-belief?

Once you catch yourself using these unhelpful thinking patterns, ask yourself the above questions to begin changing your own thoughts. Remember, the core basis of CBT is the idea that your own thoughts affect your emotions, which then influences your behavior. By catching and changing your thoughts before it spirals, you will be in control of your emotions and behavior as well.

CHAPTER 4

RECOVERING YOUR SELF-ESTEEM

As we mentioned earlier in this book, one of the most important parts that a victim or narcissism has to recover is their self-esteem. Due to the nature of narcissistic abuse, victims have a hard time accepting themselves and therefore cause them to have low self-esteem. In this chapter, we will focus on how we can use self-acceptance to help build higher self-esteem. I will also provide you with a few exercises that you can use to practice self-esteem and self-acceptance. Self-esteem is something that needs to be actively practiced, so placing priority in completing exercises is crucial. Let's take a look at what self-acceptance is and how it can help with one's self-esteem:

1) Self-acceptance is the feeling of being satisfied with yourself despite your past choices or behaviors

2) Self-acceptance is being aware of your strengths and weaknesses

3) Self-acceptance is having a realistic assessment of your capabilities, talents and overall worth

In summary of those three definitions, self-acceptance is the happiness and satisfaction that you have with yourself that is needed to achieve good mental health. Having self-acceptance means that you are able to understand who you are, be realistic about it, and be aware of what strengths and weaknesses you have. Those who have high levels of self-acceptance tend to also have a more positive attitude, do not wish to be different from who they are, accept all traits of themselves, and are not confused with their identity.

You may be wondering how all of this relates to self-esteem? Well, self-esteem is defined as having confidence in your own ability, and self-worth and self-acceptance are aware and satisfied with all your strengths and weaknesses. Self-acceptance does not need to rely on achievement to make one feel worthy. It makes people feel worthy by simply being comfortable and happy with who they are.

So how does self-acceptance work in the real world? Based on scientific studies, self-acceptance has 5 different stages. The first stage is Aversion. People's natural response to uncomfortable feelings or situation is either avoidance or resistance. For instance, if somebody dislikes a trait that they have, it is natural that they avoid it rather than dealing with it head-on. The second stage is curiosity. When aversion no longer works, people will become curious to learn more about their problems. This curiosity is the driving factor behind people looking to learn more about their problems. The more curious a person is, the more likely they are to having a fulfilling life. People who lack this curiosity tend to shy away from problems leading to get stuck in stage one, which is aversion. The third stage is tolerance. Those in this stage will wish that their problems will go away while enduring it the entire time. Many people in this stage still suffer the effects of their problems but are forcing themselves to tolerate it so they can go on with their everyday life. The fourth stage is allowing. As people's resistance slowly drains away, they then allow themselves to feel. Rather than just recognizing and tolerating, they acknowledge them and feel the emotions that occur. This is the stage of acceptance where they accept their problem and allows themselves to feel all the emotions that come with it. The fifth and last stage is friendship. During this, people begin to see the value that their feelings bring and decide to accept them rather than willing them to leave. They become comfortable enough to be friends with those feelings regardless if it's good or bad.

Examples of Self-Acceptance

In this subchapter, we will be exploring some examples of self-acceptance in practice. Those who have mastered the art of self-acceptance can look at themselves in the mirror and accept 100% of who they are. They no longer try to ignore, fix, or explain any faults or flaws that they think they have.

Self-acceptance is different for everybody. It

heavily depends on the struggles that a person has gone through and what parts of their lives that they'd rather not look at. Right below are a few examples of what other people's self-acceptance looks like:

☐ A person that is in the process of divorce feels like they have failed in life. However, this person experiences self-acceptance by realizing that they have made mistakes in their life, and their marriage has failed, but it does not make them a complete failure.

☐ A person suffering from bulimia may accept themselves as a person with an imperfect body or perception but is committed to changing their perspective.

☐ A student who studies really hard in college only to get mediocre marks can reach the point of self-acceptance where they realize that test-taking and studying may not be their strength, but this is okay because they have other strengths that they can build on.

☐ A person with low self-esteem who avoids acknowledging their self-deprecating beliefs may experience self-acceptance by first acknowledging them and realizing that not every single thought that they have is necessarily true.

☐ A worker who is having trouble meeting the goals set by their unreasonable boss might accept themselves by accepting the fact that there will be times where they won't be able to deliver on unreasonable timelines. However, they are still a good person, even if they couldn't deliver on time.

Hopefully, you were able to see the pattern in these examples. Self-acceptance is the act of realizing that although you may not be perfect in all aspects of your life, it doesn't mean that you are completely invaluable. By having self-acceptance, you are giving yourself permission to be bad at certain things but also giving recognition to the things you are good at. For a person to have healthy self-esteem, they must learn to be self-accepting and to let go of any negative judgments they have for themselves.

Using Self-Acceptance In Therapy

One of the largest uses of practicing self-acceptance

is its huge role in therapy. Research has found evidence that people who lack self-acceptance tend to also have lower levels of happiness and well-being. They often are found to have disorders like anxiety and depression. If the theory is that low self-acceptance causes low mental wellbeing, it means that high levels of self-acceptance can act as a protective factor against bad mental health. The concept of self-acceptance being the foundation of good wellbeing is the reason why self-acceptance is often incorporated into therapy.

If you have ever been to therapy, you are likely to have learned about the importance of accepting yourself and your reality. It is likely that your therapist has taught you to acknowledge all traits (good and bad) and learn to accept them. Keep in mind that self-acceptance is about the ability to accept yourself fully, and it doesn't mean that you are excusing any harmful or bad behavior. It is important that you are able to accept the truth that you have engaged in bad actions previously and you do have undesirable traits, but these are all the things that are part of being you.

This distinction is really important to make because people get confused about needing to accept themselves if they have done something awful. Accepting reality does not mean you condone it or that you like it. In the same way, accepting yourself does not mean you have to celebrate and like every part of yourself. Be able to accept the not so positive things about you is a crucial step in improving and adapting.

At the end of this chapter, you will be given multiple worksheets that will aid you in achieving self-acceptance. These are suitable for those who want to boost their self-esteem or are battling more serious problems like addiction.

Self-Acceptance Worksheet Exercises

In this chapter, we will be focusing on worksheets that will help you build self-acceptance. It is crucial that you work on these as self-acceptances is one of the cornerstones to building healthy self-esteem.

Worksheet #6.1

How Would You Treat A Friend?

The purpose of this exercise is to help you initiate compassion for yourself by treating yourself the way you would treat a friend. It's easier to be loving and forgiving to friends and family, but it is much harder to extend that same kindness to ourselves. This exercise is simple, read the questions below, and write down your answers to them.

1. Think back to a time where you had a good friend or a family member that felt down about themselves and was struggling. What was your response to your friend during this situation? Please write down what you would say and what tone you would say it in.

_____

_____

_____

_____

2. Now think back to some times where you

would feel badly about yourself. What is your response to yourself during these situations? Write down what you would say to yourself and the tone you would say it in.

_____

_____

_____

_____

3. Is there a difference between the above two situations? If there is, why is that? What factors come to mind that may lead you to treat yourself differently than the way you treat others?

_____

_____

_____

_____

4. Write down possible things that would change if you had treated yourself the same way that you would be treating someone else during a time of hardship.

_____

_____

Worksheet #6.2

Self-Compassion Bank

In this exercise, we are going to be focusing on improving your understanding of yourself and the love that you have for yourself. This exercise just requires a few minutes of your day, where you focus on showing yourself compassion.

Let's begin by thinking about a past situation in your life that has caused you stress or anxiety. Tap into that situation and see if you can feel the actual discomfort of anxiety and stress in your body.

Start to say to yourself:

"This moment is one of suffering." or "This is stressful." or "This is hurting."

Then, say to yourself:

"I am not alone." or "Other people feel this way too." or "Suffering will always be a part of life."

Now, place your hand over your heart and feel the warmth and the gentle touch of your hand against your chest.

Say to yourself:

"May I be kind to myself."

Feel free to take this exercise one step further and ask yourself, "What are the things that I need to hear right now in order to express kindness to myself?" Here are some examples:

"May I find strength."
"May I offer myself patience."
"May I offer myself the compassion that I need."
"May I offer myself forgiveness."
"May I accept myself for who I am."

Worksheet #6.3

Using Writing To Find Self-Compassion

Those who enjoy writing or prefer to express themselves through the use of words will find this exercise very helpful. This worksheet is set up into three segments and is also effective for people who aren't writers.

Follow these directions below:

Part 1:

Start by thinking about all the weaknesses you have that cause you to feel inferior. Everybody has various things that they may not like about themselves or makes them feel unequal.

Next, think about things that make you insecure. If there is one particular item that stands out to you, bring it to the forefront of your mind.

Pay attention to your feelings when focus on your

insecurity. Notice what emotions and feelings arise and let yourself experience them. People often disallow themselves to feel negative emotions, but these are all important parts of life. Negative feelings can also bring out positive outcomes such as self-acceptance.

Simply feel those emotions that arise while thinking about your insecurities. Write a blurb on the emotions that you feel:

_____

_____

_____

_____

_____

_____

Part 2:

Now that you have written about your emotions, you can begin the second part of this exercise. In this exercise, you will be writing a letter to yourself from the perspective of a sympathetic loved one or imaginary friend.

The purpose of this exercise is to show you the compassion and understanding that you often to show to your friends, to yourself.

Start this exercise by imagining a friend who is a compassionate, kind, accepting, and unconditionally loving person. Then, imagine that they share the same strengths and weaknesses as you.

Think about how this friend would think about you. They love you, they are kind to you, and they accept you. Even if you have done something to hurt their feelings, this friend is understanding and is quick to forgive.

Your friend is understanding and sympathetic, but they also know everything about your life. They know every decision that you've made to get to where you are, each step that you took in your journey, and they acknowledge all the factors that have played a role in who you are today.

Next, write a letter to yourself from the

perspective of your imaginary friend. Tailor the body of this letter on the insecurities that you have written down in part one. Think about the things this friend would say to you.

Will they tell you that your mistakes and weaknesses are unacceptable? Will they tell you that you need to be perfect? Or will they tell you that they sympathize with all the feelings you are going through?

Would they be mad at you if you feel inadequate or insecure? Will they happily encourage you to accept everything about yourself? Will they remind you of your positive traits and your strengths?

Write this letter in their perspective and make sure you are showcasing themes of kindness, compassion, and love.

Dear _____,

_____

_____

_____

Sincerely,

_____

Part 3:

When you complete this letter, take a short break and give yourself some space away from this exercise.

When you are ready to come back, read the letter you wrote with the intention to really take in what it's saying. Don't just read it as something you wrote for yourself but read it as if it really were from a friend.

Open yourself up to the sympathy and compassion that your friend is showing you. Let those words comfort and soothe you. Let those words sink in and have it turn into compassion for yourself.

CONCLUSION

First of all, I want you to congratulate yourself for picking up this book and sticking with it until the very end. It is hard to see the abuse that your narcissistic mother has done to you, and for most, this is very hard to accept and see. Some people struggle in just reading about narcissism as it brings up too many memories of pain and sadness. However, at this point, you should have a wide knowledge of what narcissism is and the sources of it in your life.

Remember, narcissism is a personality disorder, and 99% of the time, the narcissist does not realize that they have a problem. Their world has always been revolved around them and they struggle to admit fault to anything. Their lack of empathy prevents them from seeing how their actions negatively affect the people around them. Due to this, they don't see how anything they do can possibly be wrong. Now that you have learned about the science behind narcissism and the different types of it, you should identify the narcissists in your life and begin to distance yourself from them. It doesn't help that western society has become a place where it rewards narcissism. People with narcissistic personality disorders are becoming more popular than ever but you are now equipped with the knowledge of how to identify them so you can avoid inviting on into your life.

Furthermore, you studied the 16 different personality types and learned about which ones are more prone to NPD. Although this is not always true, it should give you a good idea of which types of people are more prone to it and allow you to stay away if need be. When it comes to your own narcissistic mother, it is up to you to decide what you want to do with that relationship. Some people have found success going cold turkey no contact while other people would rather keep the relationship and simply ignore her narcissistic behaviors. This choice is completely up to you and is highly dependent on how severe their narcissism is. In the second book in this series, you will learn more in depth ways of how to heal from narcissism and learning about mental disorders that are often associated with victims of narcissism.

As we learned earlier in this book, many narcissists are actively suffering from disorders like depression and anxiety. Due to their abusive treatment of their children, they also often grow up with depression, anxiety, or both. In some cases, more serious disorders like PTSD and social anxiety may arise due to the abuse. We will have the opportunity to learn about these disorders and the best treatment plans for them. Remember, there isn't anything that cannot be fixed. If you are currently suffering from abuse that's coming from your narcissistic mother, you are strong enough to escape it and begin to heal from it. However, the first step to doing all of that is understanding what narcissism is and being able to see it loud and clear within your abuser.

On top of understanding the traits and symptoms of a narcissist, you also learned about their manipulation tactics. You learned that there are numerous ways that a narcissist can manipulate someone, but their strategies usually remain consistent. Some more severe narcissists employ all of these strategies while some may only employ a few. With the knowledge that you have learned, you should be able to identify when those manipulation strategies are being used on you. Being able to identify it is more important than knowing how to escape it. If you never know that you are being manipulated, you will never be able to escape it. However, by knowing what these strategies are and what the narcissist is trying to manipulate you into doing, you may be able to deny these strategies.

We also spent some time learning about what narcissism looks like in a family environment. You learned that there are certain dynamics that only exist within a dysfunctional and narcissistic family. Children are raised with unclear boundaries and are usually never in touch with their emotions. They grow up around negativity and always feel like they are competing in order to get love and nurture from the narcissistic parent. These family dynamics are the ones that usually cause the children to suffer from multiple mental disorders in their adult life. Understanding these dynamics will help you see your own family for what it is. Children that grew up in dysfunctional families usually don't see the errors of the narcissistic parent until much later on in life. However, if you learn about these dynamics early, you will be able to identify them in your own family and decide how you want to approach it.

After that, we studied codependency and how that is very prevalent within narcissistic families. This is crucial as not many people understand the relationship between narcissism and codependency. We ended off the book by learning about the different types of narcissistic mothers and what it's like to grow up in a narcissistic family.

You are probably full of information at this point, and that is understandable. Although you may have grown up in a narcissistic environment, you probably did not truly understand the extent of how unhealthy it was. Give yourself some time to digest these topics and concepts before you try to pursue an escape and treatment plan. It is important that you understand these concepts well before figuring out what to do next. It is crucial to stay disciplined and driven in order to regain your well-being. Remember, escaping narcissism means that you will have to change your mindset forever. It probably has been this unhealthy way since you were born and it will take a lot of time and effort to completely change it into one that is healthy. However, it is a journey that will change your life for the better and open up the world to you. When you are ready, please begin the second book to learn about treatments and escaping narcissism.

CPSIA information can be obtained
at www.ICGtesting.com
Printed in the USA
LVHW021314060521
686680LV00017B/1135